Basic Rockcraft

by
Royal Robbins

illustrated by
Sheridan Anderson

LA SIESTA PRESS
1971

related La Siesta publications:

Ruth Mendenhall
BACKPACK TECHNIQUES

Walt Wheelock
ROPES, KNOTS & SLINGS FOR CLIMBERS

Walt Wheelock and Tom Condon
CLIMBING MOUNT WHITNEY

LA SIESTA PRESS
BOX 406
GLENDALE, CALIFORNIA 91209

PRINTED IN U. S. A.

ISBN 910856-34-6

{4}

Contents

Cover photo: Tom Frost leading
Roof Pitch on Salathé Wall

Introduction

What Is Rockclimbing?

A boy clambers barefoot up a tree. He does it for the pure joy of climbing; *why* doesn't matter. It is exciting. New. There is a bit of danger. The thrill of adventure in going somewhere he has never been. He might do the same on a building or on an easy, rock cliff. And from this raw beginning springs a desire to venture onto steeper walls, smoother ones. He *would* go there, but he can't—not without boots, rope, and perhaps pitons. The game becomes complex. But the point is still the same: *adventure.* For his equipment, and the development of *technique,* these things which would render his barefoot scrambles too easy, will enable him to enter more forbidden realms and so maintain that balance of exciting newness that he enjoyed on his first trip up the tree.

Historically, rockclimbing is one of the components of the broad adventure sport of mountaineering. Along with snow and ice climbing and hiking, rockclimbing is one of the methods used to reach the summit of a peak. Originally this was its only justification: it was one of the roots of the tree of alpinism. Gradually, however, it has developed into a sport in its own right, and become one of the branches of the tree, with its own twigs, shoots, and branchlets running the gamut from big wall rockclimbing such as is practiced in Yosemite Valley, through the various specialties of free and direct-aid climbing to bouldering, a gymnastic excercise close to the ground. As rockclimbing is to mountaineering, so bouldering is to rockclimbing. Originally conceived as training, it now has adherants who rarely stray more than 30 feet vertically. To the rock gymnast who specializes in bouldering, the drama of climbing high above the ground, with its potential danger and variety of demands upon the human character and abilities, mean less than the intensity and joy in the ever-finer perfecting of gymnastic moves on rock.

PURPOSE: This manual is designed to fill a gap. There is no authoritative treatment of modern rockclimbing techniques as developed in America, and especially in America's foremost rockclimbing area, Yosemite Valley. These great walls of Yosemite, its smooth slabs, awesome cracks, and fine weather, have provided an ideal ground for the perfecting of rockclimbing techniques. There has long been a need for a comprehensive description of these techniques. Yvon Chouinard's catalogue, wherein he and Tom Frost explain the use of their equipment, is excellent, but incomplete as a manual, which of course it is not intended to be. I hope this book, and the one which is to follow on advanced techniques, will help answer the growing need for such information created by the explosion in the popularity of our sport.

SCOPE: This book is intended to aid the novice in learning to climb well and safely. There is no presumption to teach him to go first on the rope. *Leading* is an art which takes time to master. The safe way to learn is through serving an apprenticeship as second man. Consequently, I have included the information and techniques which the novice will need to be an effective second, but techniques involved in leading and in climbing big walls will be discussed in *Advanced Rockcraft*.

It may well be argued that there are other ways to learn to climb, that many fine mountaineers in their early days ventured forth with a light heart and clothesline, and have, through a combination of native ability and generous quantities of luck managed to survive their rude alpine beginnings, to become seasoned and safe climbers. But this involves grave and unnecessary risks. The safer way is to stay off the sharp end of the rope until you know what you are doing.

USE: One cannot learn to climb from a book. *Basic Rockcraft* is designed to supplement instruction. It is written after nearly 20 years of personal experience using the methods described. One of the tenets of the Yosemite method is to keep things as simple as possible. This I have tried to do here. Here are ways of climbing which have been found to work, techniques which have been tested repeatedly in the severe crucible of the big walls of Yosemite and elsewhere. They are not guaranteed to be the best, but have been well tested and found useful.

A danger exists in guidebooks, a danger that the reader may rely more upon words and theories than his own common sense and instinct for survival. In my first year of climbing I did something foolish that I wouldn't have if the words of a book weren't going through my mind. I got off lightly with a broken arm and sprained ankle. Later I joined the Sierra Club and became a safer climber by climbing with men like John Mendenhall and Charles Wilts. These experiences made the booklore *real*. I recommend that the novice seek such instruction where it is available.

Learning To Climb

To become a good climber you do not need great physical strength nor superior coordination. These help, but far more important are *interest* and *will* supported by lots of energy. Nor is learning-rate a reliable indication of one's future prospects. I have seen natural climbers who were extremely apt and learned quickly, only to reach a learning plateau and cease to improve; while others who at first were downright clumsy have, through dedication, become outstanding cragsmen.

GET INSTRUCTION If possible, the novice should get the benefit of instruction from organizations, schools, or friends who are competent climbers. Attending a professional climbing school is the most efficient way to learn, but it costs money. If you cannot afford it, many outdoor organizations such as the Mazamas, the Sierra Club, the Appalachian Mountain Club, and various college climbing groups, offer instruction in rockclimbing and mountaineering. Some high schools and colleges — an ever increasing number — offer credit courses in these subjects.

PRACTICE CLIMBING The best way to sample climbing and learn the rudiments is to go with an organization or friends to a practice area. You can learn much on small rocks, and even experts may spend an entire day practicing on a 20-foot boulder. The following chapters contain information on knots, belaying and climbing. Belaying means protecting your partner with the rope, and doing it right means the difference between the rope being an agent of salvation for a falling climber and one of destruction for the entire party. So before attempting the actual climbing techniques, be sure you know how to tie yourself to the rope and that your belayer can protect you. Before starting, test the belay by yelling 'Test' and slowly applying body weight. If satisfactory, test further by climbing up a couple of feet and jumping off. Obviously, the landing must be safe, and one must be prepared for the belay to fail. If the belayer still holds you with no trouble, his position is apparently sound and you may climb without danger.

Having taken these precautions, climb up using the methods described in the chapter on free-climbing techniques. If it gets difficult, don't give up. You will never know how much you can do until you extend yourself to your limit, and you don't know that until you fall *trying*. That's the key word. Most people fall off a practice climb only after they have given up, and they never approach their real limits. Give it all you've got! You are now in the thick of the game. For novices to so push themselves, even when perfectly safeguarded, is usually difficult. If it goes too much against your nature, perhaps climbing isn't your game. Self-confrontation and inner conflict, though only part of the sport, are nevertheless an inevitable part.

If the pitch is too hard, and you fall and are lowered, don't despair; now you have a concrete goal. You have an idea of why you failed, whether it be strength, agility, technique, etc., and can work to improve that aspect of your climbing so you can return and solve the problem.

SECONDING MULTI-PITCH CLIMBS After learning and practicing the techniques of belaying and climbing, you are ready to apply them on an extended route. You must have a reliable, competent leader, and you must understand belaying and have had sufficient practice so that doing it properly is automatic. Although the leader is not likely to fall, he *could,* so his life — and yours, if you don't stop him — is in your hands. Study carefully the chapter on belaying, and practice.

On an extended climb the party moves one at a time between ledges which are used for belay stances. The area between belay stances is a *pitch,* or *lead.* While you belay, the first man climbs, placing protection if he feels its need, until he has ascended 100 to 150 feet, when he will stop on a ledge, anchor himself, and then belay you as you follow the pitch. When you arrive at the ledge, the process is repeated until the party reaches the top. If you are in the middle of a three-man party, you will first belay the leader, and then the third man. All members of the party should be well and securely anchored whenever they are not climbing.

LEARN FROM THE LEADER Watch the leader. Observe how he manages difficulties, his upright, relaxed body position, and his rhythmic movements. Note how, from a comfortable stance, he analyzes the problems ahead and moves up smoothly and without hesitation to the next resting place.

More important to watch are the ways in which the leader protects himself. When you go up second, and *clean* the pitch by removing the protection (piton, etc.) the leader has placed, note carefully his means of security: how he has hammered pitons into horizontal cracks when possible, and when forced to use a vertical crack, how he uses the wider portion of the crack, narrow above and below to prevent levering of the pin; how he sometimes uses two carabiners on one piton to lessen rope drag; how he places slings on horns and around chockstones, and study the clever placements of artificial chockstones. By watching a man who knows what he is about, you can learn much. But remember that every leader has subtle bits of knowledge which you can never possess through mere observation. It is dangerous to jump to the conclusion that you are capable of leading what you can follow. It takes time to develop the judgment and self-control needed to safely lead difficult routes.

Equipment

The beginner needs little equipment. For clothing, anything will do which is sturdy and resistant to abrasion. Tough trousers are satisfactory, but knickers are better, allowing more freedom of movement.

FOOTWEAR

Tennis shoes or hiking boots will suffice. They will allow you to sample the sport to see if it appeals sufficiently to buy more expensive gear. If so, you will eventually desire the advantages of specialized rockclimbing shoes, known as *kletterschuhe* (German) or *varappe* (French). More manufacturers are following the French lead and producing shoes with rubber along the sides and on the toe and heel. This gives better adhesion in jam cracks and protects the uppers from abrasion. Shoes without side rubber can be somewhat protected from abrasion by coating the stitching with epoxy glue.

SOLES: Some shoes come with smooth soles, some with cleated. In general, the smooth ones grip better on rough textured rock such as sandstone, while cleated ones seem to be superior on slick rock such as water-polished granite, and are certainly better for descending grassy slopes or pine-needle covered hillsides. The best rubber for general rockclimbing purposes is medium hard. Soft rubber grips well, but bends badly when standing on small edges, and wears quickly.

STIFF VERSUS FLEXIBLE: Whether one choses comparatively stiff or comparatively flexible shoes depends upon personal preference and climbing style. Stiff shoes facilitate standing on small holds and are better for most jam cracks. Flexible shoes are usually superior for rounded holds and slabs, as well as very narrow jam cracks (as they usually have a thin sole and lack a toe counter). The stiffer shoe need not fit so tightly, hence is better for approaches and descents than the flexible one which for efficiency requires a glove-like fit.

Some comparisons are as follows:

FLEXIBLE: 1) Better adhesion on sloping surfaces and rounded holds. 2) Fits narrow jam cracks. 3) Lighter. 4) Usually less expensive. 5) Allows 'feeling' the rock through the thin sole.

STIFF: 1) Better for standing on square holds or small ones. 2) Easier

on the toes for hiking. 3) Better for standing in slings in aid climbing. 4) Provides better wedge action in most jam cracks. 5) Easier transition to climbing in mountaineering boots.

No one shoe is equally good for all uses. For example, in the Shawangunks there is little friction climbing and few jam cracks. A stiff shoe is more suitable for that area. But on the rounded sandstone in the San Fernando Valley, smooth-soled, flexible shoes have been found to be better.

But ultimately, the shoe makes little difference. With a bit of practice, one can adapt to the characteristics of just about any type of footwear, though of course certain shoes will have advantages in certain types of climbing. Far more important than the efficiency of the shoe is its psychology. If you think you have the best shoe you can get for the job at hand, and if you have faith in its performance, then *that* is the shoe for you regardless of theoretical considerations.

THE ROPE For mountaineering, the advantages of synthetic fiber ropes (nylon, perlon — trade names for the same material) over natural fiber (manila, sisel, cotton, etc.) are not in dispute. So I shall not belabor the point here, except to say, *don't* use natural fiber ropes for climbing.

CONSTRUCTION — TWISTED AND SHEATH: In the synthetic ropes there are two principal types of construction. One is the time-honored twisted construction, where three or four major strands are twined around each other. Of the two, this type is less expensive — though still expensive compared to natural fibers — and has the advantage of being easily inspected for damage by twisting apart the strands to see the interior.

The other type, *kernmantle* construction, is of an outer sheath surrounding myriad long inner filaments, in some cases continuous for the entire length of the rope. Kermantle has the great advantage of sliding with less friction through carabiners and over rock surfaces, eliminating rope drag and aiding climbing efficiency. In the Alps, kernmantle is used almost exclusively, and in this country it is preferred by nearly all climbers doing long, serious climbs on rock. But when rope drag is not a problem, as in practice climbing, the lower price of the twisted rope makes it attractive.

SELECTING A ROPE: Of the various types of twisted nylon ropes available, there is some difference in strength and a great difference in handling properties. The best are those with what is called 'mountain climbing lay.' Shops specializing in alpine equipment will carry the best ropes available.

Most kernmantles sold in this country are made in Germany, Switzerland, or France. They come in a variety of bright colors which are useful when climbing with more than one rope. Some are bi-colors — half white and half red, for example. These are more expensive, but the advantage of having each half marked is considerable. Otherwise one should mark the middle with plastic electrical tape. Putting any sort of dye or chemical marking on a nylon rope is to be avoided.

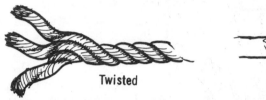
Twisted

Kernmantle

Elasticity is one of the most important properties of a nylon rope. For its ability to stretch enables it to absorb the shock of a fall far better than a natural fiber rope.

The preferred dimensions of a rope used for general rockclimbing are $7/16$" in diameter (11 mm for imported kernmantle) by 150 feet in length. In many areas a 120 foot or even 100 foot rope is adequate. Ropes of smaller diameter, say, $3/8$" (9mm) are satisfactory in strength, and are less expensive and lighter, but may be more easily cut in a fall and are more difficult to grasp when holding a weight. However, $3/8$" is satisfactory for easy mountaineering or snow climbing, and is much used for sack-hauling, and with the climbing rope in descents. A lighter rope of $5/16$" (7mm) diameter is also commonly used for these latter two purposes.

CARE OF THE ROPE: The ends should be fused and taped to prevent unravelling. The rope should be kept away from acids and solvents (gasoline, paint thinner, etc.) and stored in a cool dry place. The ultraviolet rays of direct sunlight will eventually weaken nylon. In *Ropes, Knots and Slings for Climbers,* Walt Wheelock points out that "Climbing ropes may safely be washed in an automatic washer, using a detergent recommended for nylons, and setting the heat control at 'nylon' or 'gentle action'."

WHEN TO RETIRE THE ROPE: Retire a twisted construction rope when it looks well worn. Usually this will be after three or four years of occasional weekend use, or two years of heavy use, or in extreme cases, one year. I will not climb on a twisted rope that has become so worn that it no longer has a corrugated feeling when I run my hand along it. When in doubt, throw it out!

Unless it has sustained a long fall, kernmantle can probably be used safely until the sheath wears through.

WEBBING AND SLINGS

One of the beneficial byproducts of World War II is nylon webbing. Also called 'flat rope', it has many uses in rockclimbing, among them:

SWAMI BELT: One inch nylon webbing long enough to wrap around the waist five or six times. Besides providing greater comfort in a fall or when one is hanging from the rope, this arrangement is convenient for clipping to an anchor with an auxiliary sling (umbilical cord) when not tied to the climbing rope. Also, as the climbing rope is tied directly to the Swami rather than around the body, nearly five feet of rope is saved (counting both ends).

RUNNERS: These are general purpose slings, usually made from one-inch webbing five feet long. They are used over rock horns, and around trees and chockstones as points of security. Longer runners which can double as *diaper slings* for rappels, should be about 10 feet, more or less, depending upon one's lumbar region. See chapter on rappelling.

ETRIERS: These are short rope ladders used in direct-aid climbing. The stiffer, non-tubular webbing is best as the steps in the étriers will hold their shape. But for most other uses, the soft tubular variety is better, as it is easier to work with and holds knots better.

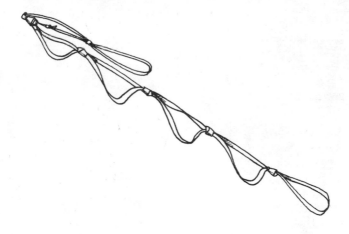

HARDWARE SLINGS: Heavy, solid, one-inch webbing is used for slings which drape over the shoulder for carrying climbing equipment. For this purpose, they are best sewn, rather than knotted, to allow the carabiners to slide easily along the length. Such stitched slings are commercially available, but are generally not recommended as runners.

SMALLER SIZES: The most commonly used smaller sizes are ½", ⁹⁄₁₆", and ⅝". Their uses will be described in the appropriate chapters.

PITON HAMMER A piton hammer should weigh from 20 to 25

ounces; a woman's, about 16 ounces. It should have a safety sling long enough to go over the head and shoulder, a flat head, and a blunt pick which can be used for prying. A good hammer is expensive, but will last five to ten times as long as a cheap one. For holsters, leather is satisfactory, but plastic is better as it holds its shape and lasts longer.

CARABINERS These are metal devices similar to big safety pins,

used to connect various elements of the climbing chain, such as rope and piton. Aluminum alloys provide the best combination of strength and weight. Most carabiners used in the United States are either of the oval shape of Raffi Bedayan's, or the modified-D shape of Chouinard's. The Chouinard carabiner has the advantage of great strength. It will hold a long fall even with the gate open. This allows them to be easily opened under body weight, helpful in artificial climbing. Unfortunately, they are more expensive than the ovals, and less suitable for carrying pitons and for carabiner brake rappels. Many climbers carry a combination of ovals and Chouinards.

When buying a carabiner, check to make sure the spring action is smooth but not too strong, that the gate meshes freely, that there are no burrs, and that they are strong. Carabiners should test to at least 2500 pounds. The responsible dealer will have information on carabiner strength. Ask *before* buying!

There are many other types of carabiners, including those with safety gates. But the two described above have been found adequate for all of the hardest climbs in our country. Anyone desiring the greater security of a gated safety carabiner can use two normal carabiners with the gates opening in opposite directions.

OVAL   CHOUINARD

carabiners & pegs on sling
photo by Liz Robbins

PITONS Pitons are pieces of metal, usually spike-like, which are driven into cracks in the rock for protection or actual aid in climbing. They come in a bewildering variety of shapes, sizes, metals, hardnesses, and strengths. They will be discussed further in the section on PITONCRAFT AND NUTCRAFT.

ARTIFICIAL CHOCKSTONES Referred to as 'nuts' or 'chocks', these gadgets are a British invention and are presently available in multiple shapes, sizes, and materials, usually metal. They can often be substituted for pitons, and are to be preferred because they do not damage the rock. More about them under PITONCRAFT AND NUTCRAFT.

BOLTS These are nail-like shafts of metal gear driven into holes drilled in the rock. Those commonly used in climbing vary in diameter from 3/16″ to 3/8″, and in length from about 3/4″ to 2½″. There are two basic types, the contraction bolt, which is squeezed together when driven into the hole, and the expansion bolt, which presses apart a surrounding sleeve. Like many of the technological wonders of modern man, bolts are at once a blessing and a curse. They make possible some of the finest rock climbs on earth by opening up stretches of blank and otherwise unclimbable rock. But they also diminish the value in climbing by making it possible for anyone to go anywhere if they are willing to drill. Bolts should *never* be placed on established routes unless the route since has been changed so it is impossible without them.

Knots

There are many knots one might use in mountaineering. We shall consider only a few essential ones. The simplest is the OVERHAND:

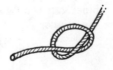

The BOWLINE is the traditional knot for attaching the end of the rope to oneself:

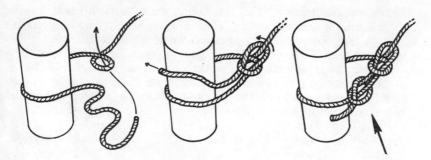

Use an OVERHAND KNOT to secure the end.

The DOUBLE-LOOP BOWLINE holds better:

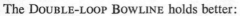

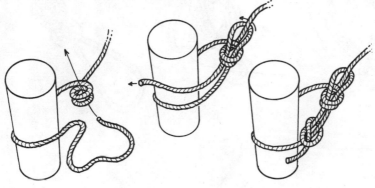

The OVERHAND LOOP is simple and useful:

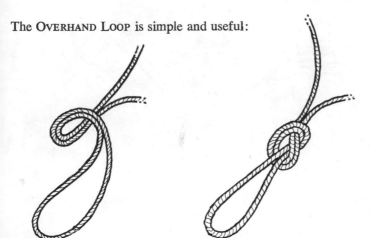

FIGURE-OF-EIGHT LOOP: This variation of the OVERHAND LOOP is easier to untie after it has held weight. Thus it makes an excellent middleman's knot. A more compicated middleman's knot called the BUTTERFLY has long been used because it weakens the rope less than other knots. However, with the great strength of modern ropes, and the small likelihood of the middleman ever placing severe strain on the rope, this precaution seems no longer realistic. The FIGURE-OF-EIGHT is simpler and should be learned anyway:

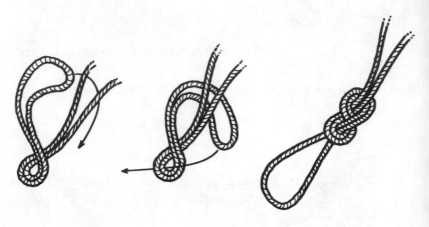

RING BEND (overhand bend, water knot) - Used for joining two ropes. Particularly good in webbing:

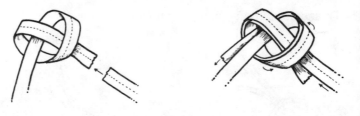

FISHERMAN'S KNOT - This is a good, safe knot for joining ropes of different diameters:

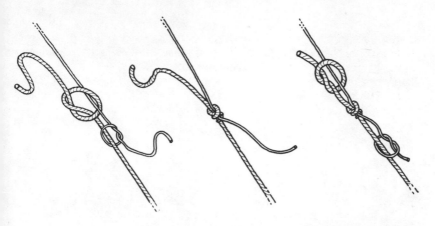

A knot which the beginner will rarely need but which can be extremely useful is the PRUSIK. It provides a means of ascending a climbing rope by using slings of smaller diameter rope. The knot will slide freely up or down on the rope but will grip solidly when weighted. If one has fallen from an overhang and is too high above the ground to be lowered, the PRUSIK might provide the only way of getting up, or at least of taking the weight off ones waist, preventing suffocation. It is a girth-hitch tied twice:

The prusik has been known to slip on badly worn ropes. Its grip can be increased by passing through the bight three times:

The best prusik slings are made from pieces of kernmantle rope, ¼" (5mm) in diameter, two to three feet long. The 5/16" (7mm) is also satisfactory, but will not grip as well as the smaller diameter.

Often, the rope will form figure-of-eight patterns while being coiled. Don't fight them. It is not worth the time required to avoid them. Before using, uncoil the rope completely into a loose pile.

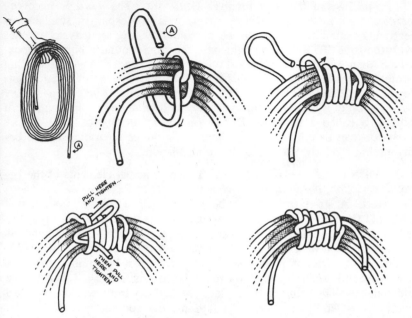

COILING THE ROPE - One hand grasps the rope about one foot from the end, and the other forms successive coils about five feet long. The finishing wrap should be made with about five feet of rope.

These knots should provide for all your needs at this time. We shall introduce a few more as we proceed, but those interested in delving further should consult Wheelock's *Ropes, Knots and Slings for Climbers.*

Belaying

How do we use the rope as a safety device rather than a lethal weapon? We had best learn this before tying ourselves to someone with the possible result of killing two persons instead of one. The event of one climber falling and pulling with him another — or perhaps several others — is not strange to the history of mountaineering. One of the most famous cases is the disaster of Whymper's party on the Matterhorn in 1865. Three men were pulled to their deaths by the fall of a fourth. The dead would have numbered seven had the rope not broken. Modern ropes are designed not to break, so now we must stop the leader or sacrifice our party.

Proper use of the rope involves BELAYING. The word is from the nautical term meaning to secure a rope to a post, spar, or similar projection. In climbing, it means one person providing security to another with the rope. To do so he might pass the rope around a hump of rock, which then becomes a BELAY POINT, or the leader may put a sling around a small tree and attach his rope to it by means of a carabiner, forming a RUNNING BELAY. The spot where one belays is a BELAY STANCE or a BELAY LEDGE. A belay without a ledge, hanging from pitons, is called a HANGING BELAY or BELAY IN SLINGS. The BELAY POSITION can be either the belay stance or the configuration of the belayer's body relative to the surrounding terrain.

ELEMENTS OF THE BELAY Three principal elements of the belay are *friction, position,* and *anchor.*

FRICTION: A strong man might be able to grip a rope in both hands and hold the fall of a light companion, but it is unwise to rely upon the mere grip of the hands in a matter of life and death. And neither that strong man nor we could ever hold the fall of a leader this way. We need help and friction is the answer. We can get it by running the rope over a round, smooth hump of rock. Unfortunately, such humps are often not available, but in their place the human torso will do. We can obtain considerable friction by wrapping the rope around the body. There are various wraps possible, but the best is around the hips. The HIP BELAY consists simply of passing the rope high around the hips and taking it in — if the climber is *coming* up — or feeding it out — if the climber is *going* up. If a fall occurs, the hand on the far side of the body from the rope leading to the climber does the holding, with the help of friction around the hips and over any rock, etc. The other hand is the guide. Do not confuse these functions in the heat of a crisis. Practice until holding with the proper hand is automatic.

POSITION: The second critical element is the position of the body relative to the direction of force in a fall. Friction is useless unless the body is braced toward the direction of pull. Usually, this means a straight leg on the side of the rope going to the climber. The belayer places himself so as to minimize any twisting action upon the body, and generally his back is toward the wall. It is not easy to judge the direction of forces in a fall, much less the extent of them. The belayer must evaluate each situation and make use of the rock to position himself most securely. Often he must be prepared for forces from various directions, as when his partner is traversing.

ANCHOR: The third element is the ANCHOR. It is our back-up if friction and position fail. Or, perhaps, if friction *works,* and position fails. A case case in point: In the spring of 1969, Don Lauria and I had just descended from the upper cliffs of Stony Point in the San Fernando Valley of southern California. We reached Little-Rock-Number-One and turned its northern corner to find a lad flat on his back, injured after a fifteen-foot fall from the top of the boulder. He had been pulled from it by the weight of a friend whom he was 'protecting' with the rope. It was his first day of climbing, and, not realizing how heavy a falling climber can be, he had failed to either position himself securely or to anchor to something which would prevent his being pulled off.

Anchoring is attaching oneself to a fixed point on the wall, whether a piton, chockstone, tree, horn, or whatever. This is commonly done by making an overhand loop in the climbing rope and securing it to the fixed point. The anchor rope should be snug on the belayer's waist, and should be arranged according to the direction of pull upon the belayer.

THE SITTING HIP BELAY Now that we have discussed the three principal elements, we shall have a closer look at using them in sitting

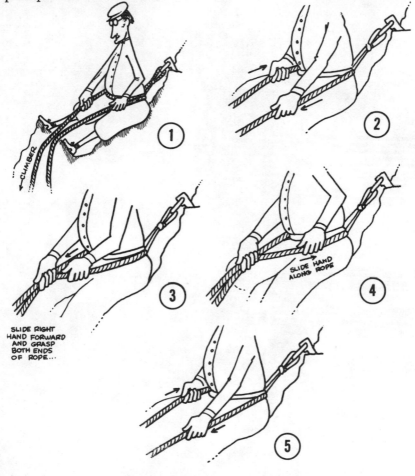

and standing hip belays. In The Soundest Position, the belayer braces his legs as well as possible against the direction of pull. The leg on the side of the rope going *to* the climber is the important one. It should be braced straight against the direction of pull as the leg bones offer better resistance than the muscles. If convenient, both legs should be so braced. The rope runs inside the knee, around the hips, and is held by the *holding* hand in front of the body. The *guiding* hand on the side of the rope going to the climber aids in taking the rope in and letting it out. The holding hand *never* releases the rope. The rope handling in the belay is similar to turning the steering wheel of a bus — the holding hand is close to the body, the guiding hand a foot or two away. As the rope is taken in, the hands move an equal distance in opposite directions. Then the guiding hand is returned to its original position where, still gripping the rope on the guiding side, it also temporarily grasps the rope in front of the holding hand, allowing the holding hand to slide back along the rope to its original position next to the waist. The belayer should arrange the belay so a fall pulls him against the rock, not away from it. In order to assure that the rope may run freely on the sturdy, trouser-protected hips, rather than the fragile, vulnerable waist, the belay rope should normally run *below* the anchor rope.

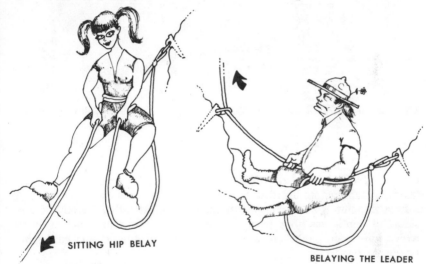

SITTING HIP BELAY

BELAYING THE LEADER

Standing Hip Belay

Here the principal of bracing the legs is the same, but is is even more critical that the leg on the side of pull be locked straight. The rope runs around the body and over the hammer-holster to insure its riding high on the hips. As with the sitting hip belay, the climbing rope usually runs under the anchor rope to keep the weight from coming on the waist. (Many belayers, however, prefer

Pratt on the Salathé
photo by Tom Frost

running the rope above their anchor line to eliminate any chance of it being pulled down over their hips. There seems to be no clear case for exclusive use of either variation.) The anchor must be snug. The *rope* runs out on the side on which a fall will pull the belayer against the rock.

BELAYING THE LEADER

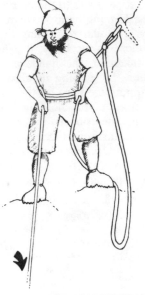

STANDING HIP BELAY

BELAYING THE LEADER If we manage the rope properly, belaying a man coming up from below presents no problems. But belaying a man going up is more complicated, so complicated that a study of considerable depth was done by members of the Sierra Club, the results of which have been published in a highly regarded little booklet called *Belaying the Leader*.

A fall by the leader is potentially serious, and may be disastrous. Therefore, it is well we prepare for it with all our attention and ingenuity. First, if a leader is only ten feet above his belayer, he will fall at least 20 feet. The belayer who can stop such a fall, when there is little or no rock intervening, is an unusual chap. If the leader falls from a mere ten feet higher, his salvation is highly unlikely. And if he falls from 30 feet above the belayer, it's "Goodby Charlie."

[28]

Falls by the leader are less serious if he has placed belay points and running belays between himself and his belayer. If, for example, the leader climbs 20 feet, places a running belay with a sling on a horn, climbs ten more feet and falls, he will plummet only 20 feet instead of 60 before his weight comes onto the belayer. And the pull upon the belayer will be upward — a much easier force to hold. But the belayer, as well as being braced toward the direction of pull, must be *anchored* away from it. A sling on a horn will not answer the question because it will not hold the belayer *down*. A piton, an artificial chockstone slotted *upward,* or a tree will provide more reliable anchors when there is a real danger of being pulled upwards off a ledge. Also, when the pull will be upward, the rope should run *under* the hammer holster.

STOPPING A FALL: In *Belaying the Leader* it was theorized that a belayer could hold a long leader-fall by purposefully letting the rope slide, braking it by degrees so as to absorb the shock. This was called DYNAMIC BELAY. To paraphrase Walt Whitman, this "proves very well in the lecture room, but not at all in the open air." George Oetzel and Randall Gardner conducted experiments on this subject, the results of which were published in the July, 1969 issue of *Summit Magazine:* "Electronic View Of Dynamic Belay." Their conclusions support the view of all the experienced climbers with whom I have discussed the subject, namely, that the forces involved in a leader fall are so difficult to judge as to render purposeful dynamic belay impractical. If the leader falls, grasp the rope as tightly as you can and hope that the built-in dynamic belay of the nylon rope (its elasticity) and fortune will save the day. If the leader really needs a dynamic belay it will be provided by the rope being ripped, willy-nilly, through your hands. Which is why so many belayers wear gloves.

Some climbing organizations conduct belay practice sessions in their local climbing areas. These involve a dummy weight of 100 to 150 lbs falling 10 feet or so. Such practice is a humbling lesson in the severity of leader falls, and is extremely valuable.

SUMMARY: Every belay situation is different. The individual must evaluate each in all its aspects and use what he has in the most effective way. Worth remembering are: 1) The anchor is all-important. 2) Brace toward the direction of pull. 3) Position yourself so the rope pulls your body toward the rock.

SIGNALS: The following are widely used:

BELAY ON — Belayer to climber. Means he is ready to protect him.

CLIMB — Belayer to climber. Said in addition to or in place of *Belay on* to more strongly indicate to his partner to come ahead.

CLIMBING — Climber to Belayer as climber starts up.

BELAY OFF — Said by either the belayer or climber. Indicates the belay either may be or is being dispensed with. Keep the belay on until the climber says *Belay off* or equivalent. This should normally be only after he is anchored.

ROPE — Climber to belayer. Short for *up rope.* Means *Take in rope,* whether up or down.

SLACK — Climber to belayer. Opposite of *Rope.* Never say *Take up slack,* when you mean *Rope.*

TENSION — Climber to belayer. Means *Hold the rope tight.* Sometimes means *Pull like hell!*

ROCK — A shout of warning similar to *Fore!* in golf. Shout it loudly upon dislodging a missile.

Direct-Aid

Direct-aid climbing (as opposed to the indirect psychological aid of a belay) is the use of pitons or other artificial aids which are attached to the rock and used physically either for progress or resting. It is also known as *artificial* climbing. While it may be artificial in a sense, in some ways direct-aid climbing is as challenging as free climbing. In any case, many of the finest climbs in the world are possible only with direct-aid methods. In the main, *aid climbing,* employing as it does, much gadgetry, lends itself more to technological solutions, whereas free climbing is more physical. Nevertheless, at their highest pitch, both disciplines require similar characteristics of control and judgement.

In leading direct-aid climbing, the primary problem is the placement of pitons or other aids. This falls within the scope of *Advanced Rockcraft.* Following artificial climbing is almost as complicated as leading, and much practice is necessary to attain any degree of smoothness and speed.

Etriers One of the tools of the aid climber is a short rope ladder known as an *étrier* (French, pronounced A-Tree-A.) These are used in pairs, with an extra carried for occasional use. In this country étriers have evolved from short two-steppers of early 1950's vintage to the present four- or five-steppers. They are made from 1" nylon webbing, but ½" webbing can be used whenever minimizing weight is important.

Aider.: This is a style of étrier especially useful for sustained aid climbing. It is made from 20 feet of stiff, solid (as opposed to flexible, tubu-

ler) 1" webbing and seven feet of the same in ½" or 9⁄16". To make
an aider, take the 1" webbing and lap one end over the other about 10
inches and make a FROST KNOT. Then tie an overhand loop which is
small but still large enough to insert a foot without struggling. Before
tying the overhand loop, lengthen one side by pulling up a bit of webbing so that a permanent loop is formed. Tie four similar, but larger and
equal loops down the length of the webbing. Now, a subsidiary étrier is
formed by tying the smaller sling to the larger. Make this 'sub-aider' by
passing the small webbing through the Frost knot and joining the ends
with a ring bend. Then, with an overhand knot, form it into two loops
the same size as the top two in the aider. The extra étrier should be made
with ½" webbing, only four steps, and no subaider. It is useful to have
several lighter étriers of this sort as they are more convenient to carry
on long climbs which have only a little aid, and hence no need for the
more specialized, bulkier, aider.

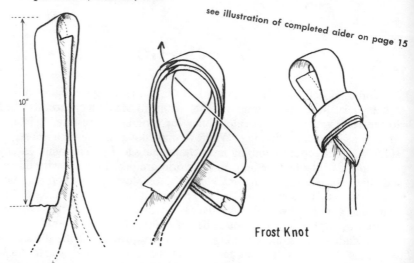

see illustration of completed aider on page 15

10"

Frost Knot

USING AIDERS: Although artificial climbing does not *require* the use of
étriers, it is much easier with them. When a leader climbs an aid pitch,
he places pitons or nuts, runs his rope through carabiners attached to
them, clips in his aiders, climbs up in them, and continues this process
until he reaches a ledge where he anchors and belays. When following
the pitch, the second man goes through a series of movements in ap-
proximately the following sequence: First he removes the climbing rope
from the carabiner. Then, he clips one aider to the carabiner on the
piton and climbs up and stands in the top or next-to-the-top rungs, one
foot in the aider and one in the sub-aider. Reaching up, he removes the
climbing rope from the next carabiner, clips his second aider to it and
steps into the most convenient rung. Standing in this étrier, he removes

all gear from the previous piton and takes it out. He is then ready to move on to the next piton and repeat the process. The most important thing to remember in this sequence to *first remove* the rope from the carabiner.

THE REST POSITION: It is most important to spare the arms. They should be used only for pulling when necessary, and then only in short bursts of action. If the wall is steep and you have to remain in an awkward position, as when removing a piton, assume the REST POSITION. To get into it, step up into a stirrup, bend the foot back and underneath the buttock and sit on your foot. The other foot is used to keep the body away from the wall. If you have trouble getting into this position, bend the knee sideways and outwards, and then down and in.

RACKING HARDWARE: Efficiency in aid climbing is greatly improved by an orderly racking of equipment on your hardware sling. Do this as you are climbing, not haphazardly clipping on pitons and carabiners, expecting to sort them later. The hardware sling is carried over the shoulder and across the chest like a bandolier. Equipment is racked on the sling according to convenience. The étriers come first, as they must be handy for instant use. For free-climbing stretches étriers can be shortened by clipping each rung-loop through the carabiner. The carabiners themselves are carried in chains of four, with the gates up and facing in. Then the pitons are clipped onto carabiners in order of size, with the smallest first. The gates of the carabiners holding pitons are down and facing out. Avoid carrying too many pitons on one carabiner as they will be difficult to remove. Five or six horizontals is about right, but angles should not exceed three per carabiner. (Three angles will ride better if the center one is reversed.) Having the large pitons in the rear will tend to push the smaller pitons forward, making them easily accessible. Following the pitons come the larger wired-chocks, and then the smaller. Next come the chocks on short slings, and finally the tie-off loops. Runners (multi-purpose slings) are carried looped over the head. Long runners can be doubled with a carabiner clipped through both loops to keep them equal. Any chocks on slings long enough to go over the head should also be carried as runners.

(see cover photo)

Pitoncraft & Nutcraft

Until after World War II, all pitons were made of iron and were sufficiently malleable to conform to the shape of cracks. Once driven, they were considered permanent fixtures. However, in 1947, John Salathe, an American who came to California from Switzerland, revolutionized piton design by using, on the first ascent of the Lost Arrow in Yosemite, hard steel pitons he himself forged from the axle of a Model-T Ford. On this five-day ascent, he and Anton Nelson re-used the same pitons repeatedly. This was a major breakthrough, for now one could do a route requiring the placement of hundreds of pitons, yet carry only 40 or 50.

Other inventive Americans followed Salathe's lead. For the first ascent of the face of Half Dome in 1957, Jerry Galwas manufactured a superb set of hard steel pitons which endured hard usage for years. Among these were angles big enough for 1¼-inch cracks. This was the first time such large pitons had been made from other than wood. These pins were designed to be driven hard, and to be removable and re-usable.

In the early 1950's, Charles Wilts invented the knife-blade piton, a peg about the size of two postage stamps and very thin. It was made of chrome molybdenum steel of high strength and resilience. Presently available *knifeblade* pitons are not as thin as the original Wilts models.

In the late 1950's Yvon Chouinard began a period of brilliant inventiveness of rock climbing (and now ice-climbing) equipment which continues today. Perhaps his single most useful contribution to the weaponry of the modern cragsman is the *RURP* (Realized-Utimate-Reality-Piton), a tiny, hatchet-faced piton designed to make use of slightly-rotten, incipient cracks in Yosemite granite. It is this piton more than any other that has opened up stretches of rock previously surmountable only by the use of bolts, an unsatisfactory solution at best. Other names prominent in the development and manufacture of American rockclimbing hardware are Bill Dolt, Ed Leeper (who invented a light, low priced Z-shaped piton of great holding power), Greg Blomberg (*CMI*) and Dick Long.

TYPES OF PITONS:

HORIZONTAL PITON: The typical piton, with eye at right angles to the blade.

VERTICAL: The simplest piton. Blade and eye aligned. Has been replaced in this country by the horizontal, which, even in a vertical crack, will hold as well or better because of torsion — a twisting effect upon the eye.

ANGLE: Once made from bars of angle stock. Formerly all angles had rings, but these are no longer used in the U. S. because of their susceptibility to damage and the potential weakness of the weld. The smallest angle piton fits a ½"-crack, the largest, a six-inch crack.

BONGS: Angles more than 1½" wide are *bongs*. They are made of steel or aluminum, and commonly are riddled with holes to reduce weight. Bongs larger than 3½-inches are rarely used.

KNIFEBLADES:
RURP: For direct aid only.

Other types of pitons will be covered in *Advanced Rockcraft*.

PLACING PITONS: The placement of pitons is normally the function of the leader, and since a discussion of leading is beyond the scope of this book, we shall cover this subject only briefly.

Ideally, a piton should be inserted into a crack ½ to ⅔ of its length and driven hard to the hilt. A ringing sound, steadily increasing in pitch, usually indicates a solid piton. Another test is to tap the hammer lightly against the side of the head of the pin. If the piton doesn't give, and if the hammer bounces with a good spring, it's probably good. But these tests are not completely reliable. Expert climbers avoid trusting their luck to one piton, no matter how tight it seems. When there is a choice, select a honizontal crack over a vertical.

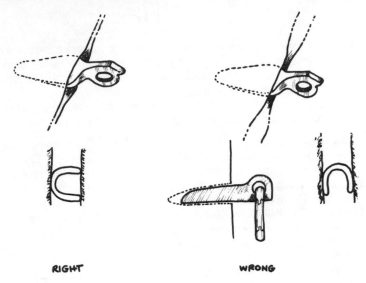

RIGHT   WRONG

A piton driven straight up, or upward at an angle, is not necessarily bad, especially when it is long and driven well.

When placing a piton in a vertical crack make use of any variations in the shape of the rock to cradle the piton and hold it in place. A slightly wider part of the crack which narrows above and below will hold a piton better than a flush crack, or a part of the crack where the sides are both convex.

Be alert to the character and formation of the rock. Rock which appears solid may be unstable. Avoid driving pitons behind loose flakes and blocks.

REMOVING PITONS: To remove pitons, hit them back and forth until loose and then pluck out. If possible, aim the blow at the heftiest part of the neck of the piton, or at least at the top of the eye. Horizontal pitons are best knocked as far as possible in each direction, but with

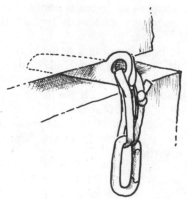

angles it is better to knock them only a short distance each way and so create a groove. Remove angles by hitting them high on the neck. Often, for this purpose, the blunt pick end of the hammer works better as it can be directed more accurately.

Sometimes it is possible to hit the piton downward far enough to bring the hammer to bear directly on the bottom of the eye.

EXPANDING FLAKES: The removal of pitons from behind expanding flakes is a special problem. Here are some solutions: 1) Pry it out with the pick of the hammer. When prying, hold one hand over the top of the piton, ready to catch it. 2) Vigorously jerk it back and forth with a sling. 3) Widen the crack with the tip of a larger piton. 4) Pull outward on the piton while knocking it back and forth. Rather than destroy a crucial flake to remove a piton, leave it permanently fixed.

Bongs can often be removed by reaching inside the crack and hitting outward.

To avoid dropping the piton, have a hand ready to catch it when it becomes loose. If this is not possible, clip a carabiner onto it when it has become loosened, and use the pick end of the hammer to avoid hitting the carabiner. Alternatively, one may carry an old carabiner and use it as a piton keeper, but this means carrying an extra piece of gear. Develop the art of piton removal so that hundreds of pitons can be removed and none dropped.

ARTIFICIAL CHOCKSTONES These were first invented and used in Britain from the British habit of using natural chockstones for runners. The second step was to carry a pocketful of pebbles and insert them into cracks. Then began the use of regular machine nuts with slings through the holes, which led to present-day artificial chockstones in their variety of designs, shapes and sizes. The use of these chocks in the United States is a comparatively recent phenomenon, but is steadily gaining momentum.

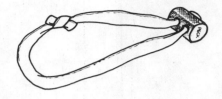

WHY USE CHOCKS? Chocks are becoming popular for a number of reasons. They sometimes give excellent protection when it is impossible to place good pitons, as when one is working with loose rock or expanding flakes. Sometimes they are faster to place than pitons and usually faster and easier to remove. Also, the satisfaction to be gained from using them is to be weighed. For many this is great: the silent communion between man and rock, the feeling that one is *with* the rock, the greater sensitivity to its minute variations and configurations, the knowledge that one is not violating the rock, smashing it with pitons. However, the greatest service chocks provide is in allowing us to protect some climbs, and parts of most climbs, without the aid of pitons. With the growing numbers being drawn to the sport, our American ethic of removing pitons to keep the route 'pure' is beginning to yield diminishing returns. A route on which the cracks are scarred and powdered, and the rock broken and loose because of the continual placement and removal of pitons, is scarcely in its natural state. There is little to choose from between a route in this condition and one studded with pitons. Chocks have the great virtue of being removable points of protection which do not damage the rock.

A chock is placed in a narrowing section of a crack where it will resist a downward pull by wedging. It can be wedged more firmly by a sharp downward pull on the sling or a light tap with the hammer. Chocks should be placed with consideration given to ease of removal, which is usually done by jerking upward on the sling. However, some wedge-shaped chocks are difficult to remove by pulling, and it is best with these to remove them with the fingers. A long horizontal piton is useful in lifting out chocks deep in cracks. Firmly wedged chocks may be loosened by placing a piton on their underside and hitting upward.

Rappelling

Rappelling is a means of descending by sliding down a rope. Usually the rope is doubled, allowing retrieval by pulling one end, thus the French word, *rappel,* meaning: to recall.

METHODS There are many ways of rappelling. The aim of all is to provide enough friction so the body can be lowered slowly and in control.

THE DULFER: This is the classical method and the one to learn first. Straddle the rope facing the anchor point. Bring the rope around the left hip, across the chest, over the right shoulder and down across the back to be held in the left hand. This is the braking hand, and the right is used mainly for balance. (These directions, of course, can be completely reversed.) When learning to rappel, use the protection of an upper belay. It is best to begin on a slope of about 60 degrees. Slowly back down, balancing with the upper hand and braking with the lower.

The upper body leans out somewhat so the feet press in toward the rock. Do not allow the feet to get too high or you will run the risk of turning upside down. As you become more proficient, steepen the angle. The rappel should be smooth, with sudden, jerky stops avoided, as these place an unnecessary load on the anchor. A freewheeling, bouncing, fast rappel is OK for the expert who has an absolutely reliable anchor, but is more of a stunt than a working rappel.

DULFER WITH SEAT SLING: The classical Dulfer has the virtue of simplicity, but unless properly padded is hard on the seat and shoulder. Using a sling and carabiner takes the pressure off the seat, making it necessary to pad only the shoulder. A serviceable seat-sling can be fashioned from a simple runner by making it into a figure-eight and putting one leg through each hole. The carabiner is clipped to the cross in the figure-eight and the rope runs through it instead of around the hips.

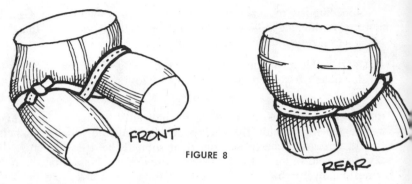

FIGURE 8

Otherwise this method is the same as the Dulfer. For safety it is best to use two carabiners with gates set in opposite directions.

A better seat sling is the DIAPER SLING, made from a runner about 10 feet long, more or less depending upon hip size. This sling fits the hips like a diaper, the three loops held not by a safety pin, but a carabiner, or preferably two.

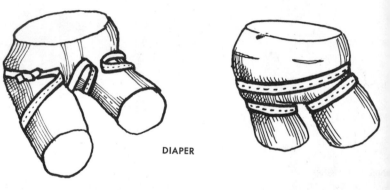

DIAPER

A seat sling can be prevented from sliding downward when scrambling between rappel points by clipping one of the carabiners to the swami belt.

DULFER WITH SEAT SLING

CARABINER BRAKE RAPPEL

CARABINER BRAKE RAPPEL: With the seat sling Dulfer (modified Dulfer) one still is faced with the problem of absorbing the energy of the rope going over the shoulder. There are various rappelling devices which will do this, but they require carrying an extra item of equipment, and this is to be avoided unless the advantages are great. As with the modified Dulfer, a seat sling is necessary for the carabiner brake rappel. Two carabiners, with gates turned in opposite directions, are attached to the sling, and to these are attached two more with their gates also reversed. As illustrated, two more carabiners cross the second pair and the rappel rope forms a bight over them, providing most of our friction. The rope is held in the left or right hand and braked as needed on the same side.

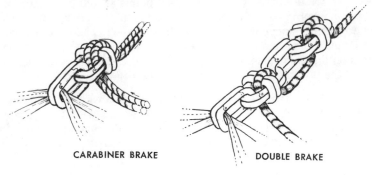

CARABINER BRAKE   DOUBLE BRAKE

To gain additional friction, pass the rope around the hips and brake with the hand on the other side of the body. The hand not used for braking is normally used for balance on the rappel rope above the body. Some additional friction can be gained by using three cross carabiners, but if one is making a steep rappel on two thin ropes or on a single rope, greater friction can be achieved by making a double carabiner brake rappel.

Caution: Although the carabiner brake rappel is more comfortable than the other methods mentioned here, it has the serious drawback of being complicated. Fatigue, darkness, or speed can lead to a faulty arrangement of carabiners and danger of accident. Each time, before descending, double-check the elements of the system to see that all is well.

MULTIPLE RAPPELS Any of the above methods can be used to make a single rappel or a series of them to get down from a mountain. Some of the things said below apply as much to single rappels as to multiple ones, especially the points about anchors.

ANCHORS: Of all the elements in the rappel, the most critical is the ANCHOR. All depends upon this one point, and, as most rappel accidents happen through failure of anchors, it is well to devote much attention to properly setting them up. The simplest rappel anchor is a tree or horn of rock around which the rope can be passed. Or, to make the rope easier to pull down, slings can be placed around the object and the rope passed through them. Another good reason for doing this is that repeated retrieval of rappel ropes from around small trees will injure and eventually kill them. If a rock knob is used it must have a deep enough notch to prevent the rope or sling slipping off. It is always best to use two slings, so that if one fails the other is there to back it up. For the same reason, when using artificial chockstones, pitons, or even bolts for anchors, place two or more. Sometimes one must trust all to one point of security, but this is to be avoided when possible. However, on a big mountain — where speed is essential, rappels many, and the equipment one can carry minimal — the greater danger of single point rappels must often be accepted.

TESTING ANCHORS: Any suspect rappel points should be tested. Do this by first anchorng to some reliable point (such as the rappel rope coming down from above if a rappel has been made). Then clip a runner to the rappel point, step into it, and bounce vigorously. This will put more stress on the point than a smooth, slow rappel. If there is further doubt, all but the last member of the party can be belayed.

TOSSING DOWN THE ROPE: Normally one rappels with the climbing rope knotted to a light hauling line (7mm or 9mm) with a ring bend or fishermans knot. The ropes should be carefully uncoiled into a pile, and, after passing the smaller rope through the anchor sling and joining the two, we are ready to throw the ropes off and rappel. Care should be used in doing this, because if the rope is thrown off in a mass of coils, it will often snarl. A good method is to make a hand coil of about half the rope starting from the knotted end, and toss this off first. Then coil the remaining rope to the end and throw it down. Even this method is not certain, and sometimes the first man down must unsnarl the rope.

THE DESCENT: The first man descends using one of the three methods described above. If there is any doubt about his security, he should be belayed. If a belay is impractical a prusik knot can be tied around the doubled rope and attached to the swami belt. The prusik is kept loose and open with the balancing hand, but tight enough to grip in case of an accident. When using a carabiner brake, safety can be increased by tying a hefty knot in the end of the ropes, say a figure-eight loop with the doubled ropes. If the knot is bulky enough, it will not be able to pass through the carabiners, and will thus prevent one from going off the end of the rope. When the first man reaches the end of the rappel and is on a ledge, the first thing to do, before detaching himself, is to *anchor*. When securely anchored, he disengages from the rope, shouts "Off rappel," and the others come down. The last man should make sure, as he comes down, that the rope does not run into any crevices where it may jam when being retrieved. He should also assure that the ropes are kept running straight and do not twist around each other. Retrieval of the rope will be easier if the smaller rope is passed through the rappel point.

If there is any possibility the rope might be difficult to retrieve, it should be checked before the last man starts down.

SPECIAL CAUTIONS In using rappels involving carabiners or other devices, be careful lest clothing or hair slip into the system. This is a very real and constant danger.

Most kernmantle ropes elongate less under low loading than do twisted ropes. If one is using a 5/16-inch twisted rope with an 11mm kernmantle, the twisted rope will stretch far more during the rappel, causing the weight to come more and more onto the kernmantle until the force is equalized by the twisted rope *shifting around the rappel point*. If the rappel rope goes through a nylon sling, it could cut it. The use of rappel rings eliminates this problem, but involves carrying an extra piece of equipment and adding an unnecessary link to the chain. The best solution is to rappel with ropes of similar elongation.

DOUBLE-UP AND DOUBLE-CHECK There are over a dozen ways "to get the chop" rappelling. The rappel rope can break, or the knot can come untied. The sling attached to the piton can break or come untied; the piton can break or pull out. These are a few of the possibilities. By doubling up whenever possible on the failure points (e.g. using two pitons, two slings, etc.), and by using reliable equipment (e.g. ropes in

good condition), and by double-checking the elements of the rappel system (e.g. the knot on the seat sling), one can reduce to insignificance the risk of rappelling.

Face Climbing

Face climbing is the classic form of climbing on rock. It is similar to climbing a ladder. The legs do the heavy work, the arms are used for balance and to help maintain a vertical posture. It would be difficult to ascend a ladder with the body pressed against it. Yet many novices climb this way on rock. And for a very natural and understandable reason: they are scared. And as the steepness of the rock increases, so does the instinct to lie against it. Unfortunately, this greatly impedes progress, reduces our scope of vision, and often causes an outward pressure on the feet, increasing the chance of their slipping. Standing straight is mainly a matter of confidence, which will slowly increase as our experience does. But it will help at first to make a conscious effort to keep the body upright.

An idealized ladder situation is rarely found, but similar formations are. The difference is the steps are not always conveniently spaced. There are gaps. To bridge these we use various methods which form the body of our *technique*. The more subtly the rungs of the ladder are connected, the better must be our technique to piece them together.

HOLDS: The first element of technique is the use of holds. They come in an infinite variety of sizes, shapes, and angles, but the basic form is the CLING HOLD, which as the name implies, is something to which one *clings*. It usually takes the form of a square-cut ledge which if large enough is a HANDHOLD, or if smaller, FINGERHOLD. Such ledges are even

better when cut downward and inward, and are then sometimes called THANK-GOD HOLDS, or BUCKETS. Square ledges which are cling holds for the hands, form the classic type of FOOT-HOLD, or TOE-HOLD.

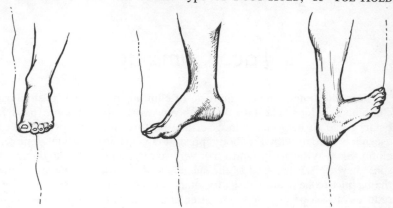

Usually, the best part of the foot to use on a toe-hold is the upper, outside edge of the big toe. But if one is wearing flexible shoes, it will often be better to cover the hold with the bottom of the sole and then twist the foot so the side of the shoe next to the rock is forced down and inward on the hold. This is called SMEARING. If the ledge slopes downward and *outward,* it becomes useless as a cling hold, but may still be valuable as a PRESSURE HOLD. These are used by pressing downward with the heel of the hand on the sloping surface. It usually works best to have the elbow pointed upward and the fingers angled toward each other. Sloping ledges, if not too steep, may provide adequate footholds also. It is important that the ankle be flexed to allow the sole to remain flat against the rock, providing a better grip.

OPPOSITION HOLDS: These are holds which, for the most part, are the same as those of which we have already mentioned, except that they involve one part of the body working against another part, creating a vector of forces which neutralizes that of gravity. One of the simplest is the

PINCH GRIP. This involves pinching a ridge of rock with the hand. In this case the thumb works against the fingers. In a variation of this hold, the fingers are inserted with the thumb downward into a thin crack, and pull against the edge in one direction, while the thumb pushes against the opposite wall of the crack. The LIE-BACK HOLD is another opposition hold. It is like a cling hold turned on end. The fingers grasp it and pull in one direction, while the feet or a foot push in the opposite. The UNDERCLING is similar, except that the hands pull upward, while the feet

press down. Still another opposition hold involves inserting the hands into a crack and pulling against the walls in opposite directions. This is commonly used in shallow, sloping gullies, rather than on steep walls, as the amount of force one can generate in this fashion is small.

COMBINATION HOLDS: Often one uses a combination of holds. An example is one hand pulling on a cling hold, and the other pushing on a pressure hold. Or, one might keep a foot on a steep, sloping shelf by pulling outward on a lie-back hold, or by pushing upward against the opposite wall of a gully. The combinations are limitless. Keep your mind open to any ways, strange and unorthodox though they may seem, which will contribute to the central purpose — overcoming the pull toward the center of the earth.

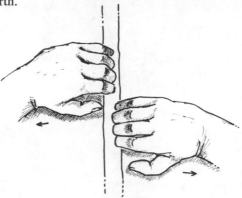

JAMMING: It is possible to climb without holds as we normally think o. them, by wedging or jamming our body or parts of it in a vertical crack. Of all the free climbing techniques, jamming is the most difficult to learn; first, because it is strenuous and more important because it is totally foreign to our experience. Cling holds are understandable. Here is something one can grab. But jamming must be deliberately learned and fostered.

For ease of understanding we can divide jamming technique into *wedging* and *opposite pressure*. Wedging in its purest form is illustrated by a chockstone in a crack. It is lodged because the walls of the crack are closer to each other below than they are above the stone. The boot or fist can function as a chockstone if the crack is the right width and the narrowing sufficiently abrupt. On the other hand, the human body, not rigid like a stone, is capable of exerting pressure against the walls of the crack sufficient to overcome the pull of gravity even if the crack is wider below than above. Most often the two elements of wedging and pressure will be used together.

TYPES OF JAMS

FINGER JAMS: In narrow cracks, say ½ to 1 inch wide, the middle joints of the fingers may be wedged. Often, it is best to turn the hand so the thumb is down, as this will provide better opportunity for twisting action giving pressure with fingers in addition to the wedging action.

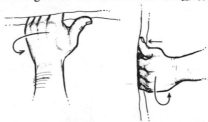

HAND JAMS: There are many types of hand jams, but the basic one is a sort of chockstone-like wedge developed by the great English climber, Joe Brown. This is formed by placing the thumb diagonally across the palm. The hand thusly shaped can be inserted into a crack like a chockstone and jammed just above the wrist. In narrower cracks the thumb must remain vertical along the side of the hand, but the wedging action can be helped considerably by pressing hard with the finger tips against one wall of the crack. Another type of hand jam is the FIST JAM, whereby the hand is doubled into a fist and inserted with the palm toward the back of the crack. This jam requires crack of just the right dimensions, and uses the muscle strength of the hand more than the others. It is generally less secure than the regular hand jams.

FOOT JAMS: The essence of the foot jam is a twisting action of the foot achieved by dropping the knee to the side and inserting the foot sideways, and then moving the knee to a vertical position. If one cannot actually insert the toe because the crack is too narrow, a similar action with the edge of the toe along the outside of the crack will help. The toe can often be at least partially jammed into right angle corners, even though no crack exists. Here the toe should point upward and the foot flex at the instep to provide continuous pressure inward toward the back of the corner.

WIDE CRACKS: Cracks four to six inches wide are the worst size for jamming, because they are too wide to get effective jams with either the hands or the feet, yet are too narrow to get the body inside to wedge. Jamming in such cracks is generally done by a combination of opposite pressure techniques and occasionally jamming the knee. It is complicated and very strenuous. A typical method of climbing such a crack is: Assume the left side of the body is toward the rock. The left arm is inserted into the crack and opposite pressure gained by pressing the heel of the hand against one wall and the elbow against the other; the left foot is inserted at knee level with the toe pressed sideways against one wall and the heel sideways against the other; if possible it is helpful to wedge the knee; the right hand either pulls against the side of the crack or pushes down against the side; and the right foot gains purchase similar to the left but at the edge of the crack, or by pointing the toe down and the heel up and wedging against opposite walls. In practice many variations of this technique can be found to aid in the struggle.

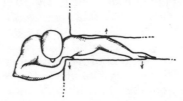

CHIMNEYS AND SQUEEZE CHIMNEYS: A chimney is a crack wide enough to accept the body. A squeeze chimney is one *just* wide enough. The easiest to climb is about three feet wide. Here, the legs and arms work in alternating scissors-like fashion. The legs are drawn up beneath the body, and the feet pressed against opposite walls. As the legs are extended, the body moves upward, and then the arms support the body while the legs again retract. In a variation of this technique, the leg in front of the body (the left, say) sustains the position after the legs have been extended and the right leg is also placed in front, but higher, and holds the body while the left leg moves to the rear for another scissors action.

squeeze chimney
photo by Liz Robbins

If the chimney is wider, the feet remain in front. The body is moved upward by pressing down with the hands in back. In very wide chimneys it is possible, especially if a few holds exist, to bridge the gap with one foot and hand kept on one side and the other foot and hand on the other side, nothing else touches the rock. If the crack is narrower, progress is more difficult and many variations come into play. Typically, wedging is achieved as follows: the knees are splayed against the wall in front, while the feet, buttocks, and shoulders are pressed against the rear wall. The hands are used by pressing the palms, fingers down, against the front wall. Progress is managed by a sort of rocking motion, raising first one knee and buttock, and then the other.

As the crack becomes ever more narrow, the body is forced into a more nearly vertical position, allowing less power in opposite pressuring. Two techniques are especially useful here. One is the TOE-AND-HEEL FOOT JAM, whereby the toe is pointed downward and pressed against the far wall and the heel pressed against the back wall. In this technique, big feet and stiff shoes help. The other technique is more difficult to manage without considerable practice. It is the elbow lock which I developed in the late 1950's to provide greater security in squeeze chimneys. It works on the same principal as the toe and heel jam. The elbow is equivalent to the heel of the foot, and the heel of the hand functions as the toe of the foot. With a bit of practice, the entire body can be easily suspended from the elbow lock. Practice is necessary to gain the shoulder agility to manage this technique. It is the same shoulder agility needed in mantling. If the crack becomes more narrow, it will not accept most of the body and becomes a wide jam crack, which we have already discussed.

Other Techniques

THE LIE-BACK: This is another method of ascending a wall by using a vertical crack. It is especially useful in corners. The hands grasp the edge of the crack and pull while the feet press against the wall in front. The hands and feet are then moved alternately upward in small stages. The arms should be kept extended so the bones rather than the muscles do most of the work. The feet must be kept high to assure they don't slip, but keeping them too high is unnecessarily taxing on the arms. The art of lie-backing is to maintain just sufficient pressure without straining more than necessary. But one can't do this without the ability to relax. And this ability comes from confidence which only experience can provide. In any case, lie-backing is strenuous, so before launching into one, know just where you are going, and then move deliberately and rapidly.

BRIDGING: Bridging is spanning a gap with the body, usually by having one foot on one side and one on the other. It is particularly useful in climbing right angle corners when holds exist on either wall of the corner. One bridges the corner by putting a foot on either wall, thus combining chimney-like opposite pressure with face climbing. This permits greater freedom of movement and vision, and the opposite pressure created by the legs working against each other makes optimum use of the holds. Bridging is, however, psychologically difficult because one does not have to look backwards to see *down*. Very often on rock features other than dihedrals, a modified form of bridging can be extremely valuable. One does well to be especially alert for bridging opportunities because of our built-in psychological reluctance to consider techniques or holds which put us into more exposed, but probably safer and more advantageous positions.

SLAB CLIMBING: In this country, slab climbing was formerly called *friction climbing* until it was realized more clearly that true friction climbing is rare. Slab climbing is low angle face climbing. If the angle is sufficiently low, no holds are necessary and we have true friction climbing. Progress is made by keeping the palms and soles flat on the rock, with the body, especially the hips, as far away from it as possible. As the angle increases, we must select surface undulations to give a more firm purchase for hands and feet. Very slight variations will make a great difference, and we make use of tiny ledges and flakes which would be dismissed from consideration on a steeper wall. These holds can be used as cling holds or pressure holds, though as the slab steepens we use them more and more as cling holds. Slab climbing is a special art different from face climbing and crack climbing. Strength is less important, though strong fingers and sturdy foot muscles help. The expert slab climber is distinguished by grace and a cool mind. He keeps his weight over his feet and moves calmly and deliberately, as if he were only a foot off the ground. He does not rush. He looks ahead, carefully calculates his tactics, and acts with resolution. His footwork is neat and deft, for he realizes the importance of precise use of holds. And he concentrates totally on the problem in front of him.

MANTLING: This is a way of raising the body by pressing downward with the arms, and is especially useful in getting onto a ledge when there are no holds above.

heel-and-toe jam
photo by Liz Robbins

CLASSIC MANTLE: In the simplest mantle the palms are placed about a foot apart chest high on a flat ledge. With a coordinated movement, the body springs upward to be supported by the extended arms pressing straight downward. A foot is lifted to the ledge and one stands up. A basic requirement is sufficient agility to raise your foot to the ledge.

MANTLING ON LEDGES ABOVE ONES HEAD: This is more difficult, but proper technique will help. Grasp the ledge with both hands and walk the feet up the face as far as possible. Then, with a quick movement, flip one elbow up so the heel of the hand is pressing straight down. With another quick movement, flip the other elbow up the same way and press up into the extended position.

SPECIAL MANTLES: Especially difficult are those mantles on very sloping or very small ledges, or onto good ledges with overhanging rock beneath. Considerable arm strength is required, as well as considerable shoulder agility. We are here moving into the realm of the expert and of the rock gymnast, but a few notes on the basic points are in order. Assume we have a sloping shelf about chest high. First of all, inspect for any depressions or bumps. Then place the heels of the hands on whatever rounded or sloping holds exist. The elbows are pointed upward, the fingers toward each other. Now the idea is to get the weight of the body over the holds and press upward into the extended mantle position. A key to these difficult mantles on poor holds is to fit the hand just right on the hold, so that it won't slip off when the arms are extended. The critical part of the palm is the small, protruding bone next to the wrist on the side away from the thumb. This bone, and the meaty part of the palm running between it and the small finger, must as far as possible be *hooked* onto whatever small bump or rugosity exists. Considerable practice may be necessary to loosen the muscles of the shoulders so the elbows can be placed high and forward as they must be in order to push straight down.

HAND TRAVERSES: We have shown under Mantling how one can grasp a ledge above and walk the feet up a blank face. It is possible to use this 'walking' technique in other ways, as for example to get the body high enough to reach a good hold. It is also possible to move sideways across a blank section if one has a good ledge for the hands. Then we have the HAND TRAVERSE. Don't let the legs dangle. Use the feet. Hand traverses are even more strenuous than lie-backs, and the same cautions about moving deliberately and rapidly apply.

CLIMBING DOWN: It is this art, more than anything else that is likely to get one out of a tight spot. But as it is more difficult than going up, and as we get little opportunity to do it as a matter of course, it is well to practice it whenever possible. The technique is much the same as going up, and the main problem is in seeing where one is going. On easier terrain, face out and use the palms for pressure holds, but as the going gets more difficult, it is best to turn sideways and finally to face the rock when necessary. To aid vision when facing in, keep the body well away from the rock.

Other Elements

We have discussed types of holds and how to use them, pressures, the importance of keeping the body vertical and away from the rock, and the various techniques. There are other elements which must be joined with the foregoing to increase the skill and ease with which we can move up rock.

RHYTHM: Foremost among these is smoothness and fluidity in our movements. As with keeping the body vertical, this will tend to come naturally as we gain confidence in our ability, but it can be nurtured by a conscious effort to move with a bit of spring. Rhythm eases the muscular effort and saves our strength, and the amount of strength one is able to conserve is far more important than the amount of strength one has. Basically, it is like the difference between placing a foot on a chair and pulling up totally with the force of one leg or making the effort much easier by giving a bounce with the other foot.

LOOKING AHEAD: Usually, difficult sections are interspersed with easy bits and resting places. Rest where you can and study the rock ahead. Though not always completely successful, the effort to climb the next section with the mind before attacking with the body is better than rushing on blindly and being caught in an awkward position not knowing where the next holds will be.

RESTING: It is important to stop between strenuous sections to regain strength. Often this is an art requiring ingenuity and experience, and on many difficult routes discovering ways to rest is as much a part of the problem as the actual climbing. One may sometimes find ingenious ways of using opposite pressures to take the weight off the arms. The ability to relax is also important, and this again is hard to achieve without the confidence which comes from experience.

USING THE LEGS: The large muscles of the legs are far more suited for propelling the body upward than are the arms. Use them whenever possible and save the arms for points of balance and security, rather than levers for pulling. One of the commonest mistakes of the novice is gripping the rock as if he would squeeze nectar from it. His strength quickly ebbs. Learning to conserve his strength, to hold on no tighter than necessary, is one of the key elements of free climbing, especially of leading. But it is an art which takes time to develop.

LOOSE HOLDS: Loose rock is a subtle and treacherous enemy lurking in the most unlikely places. A moment's carelessness can undo a lifetime of caution. All handholds should be tested by striking with the heel of the hand; foot-holds by kicking. It is impossible to tell whether a hold is solid by looking at it. Often a loose hold can be used by pulling straight downward, rather than outward.

PRACTICE: The best way to learn to be at home on rock is climb-climb-climb. The nuances of technique required to meet the subtle differences in each situation are far too numerous and fine to catagorize and put in a textbook. All we can do is show the rough outlines.

Ethics & Style

ETHICS

Actions which directly affect others in the climbing community are properly questions of ethics. Several might be considered, but we will be concerned with only one.

PRESERVATION: The primary ethical consideration involves leaving a route unchanged so others may enjoy, as nearly as possible, the creation of those who made the first ascent. Through the years there has been controversy over questions of placing and removing bolts, as well as other questions such as destroying holds or creating them with the pick end of the hammer. Those removing bolts (and holds) often think everyone should do a route in the best possible style or not at all. This is extreme.

photo by Liz Robbins

Climbing in good style is admirable, but must everyone be forced to do so? Opposing these super-purists are extremists of the opposite bent who insist all routes should be accessible to all persons. A compromise is in order, one based upon a simple point of reference.

THE FIRST ASCENT PRINCIPLE: A climb is a work of art, a creation of the men who made the first ascent. To make it more difficult by chopping bolts is to insult those who put it up and to deprive others of the joy of repeating the route as the first party did it. It is like taking anothers painting or poem and 'improving' it. Better to paint our own pictures and write our own poems. On the other hand, to bring a climb down to one's level by placing bolts (or pitons on an all-nut climb) shows an equally lamentable lack of respect for, and degrades the accompishments of, its creators. If we do not disturb the route done in a shoddy manner (e.g. the placement of unnecessary bolts), it will do no harm, and may provide a good climb for the less capable. And as for the route done in elegant fashion — let it remain as a pinnacle of achievement to which we may aspire. Better that we raise our skill than lower the climb. So let it be.

The above definition of climbing ethics, self-limiting as it is, has the advantage of avoiding the chancy area of pre-judging the way a *first ascent* should be done. This is left entirely to the individual and becomes a question not ot *ethics* but of *style*.

STYLE

'Style' is a slippery word, difficult to define. In rockclimbing it refers to the methods and equipment used, and the degree of 'adventure' involved in the ascent. Adventure here means the degree of uncertainty as to the outcome. Generally, methods and equipment determine the amount of adventure. Thus, by using the method of siege climbing (returning repeatedly to inch fixed lines higher and still higher) and using as part of our equipment an unlimited number of bolts — success on any pure rock climb on earth, no matter how flawless, is virtually assured. There would be no adventure in such an endeavor, and it would be in the worst possible style. On the other hand, to assault a great wall in a direct, committing way, without fixed lines, and with a limited amount of food, water, and equipment, is to climb in good style. It is to place more trust on one's personal qualities and skill, and less reliance on equipment and laborious methods. But the style must be suited to the climb. To use good big-wall style on a little wall is to turn good style to bad. To climb in good style is to climb in the most natural way possible, to do it with the smallest number of technological aids. The first technological aid to be eliminated, if possible, is the bolt, for it can be placed anywhere. With pitons one at least needs a crack, though almost any size and shape will do. Jammed nuts are better, for with them we must adapt to the nature

PROPER

IMPROPER

of the crack. We must work *with* the rock; we can't force it. It is more natural. Better still are runners placed on the natural belay points such as horns, trees, or chockstones. And finally, we come to climbing alone, without a rope. But that will be for the few. The trick is to suit the style to the climb and to oneself. The truly ultimate style is the perfect match — the treading of that fine edge between ambition and ability.

Granted we are free to try to climb in any style we choose as long as we don't damage the route, what about the many individuals who desire

a better definition of the *good game,* those who aren't so much interested in getting up routes as in meeting the essential challenge of them? What is a good general goal to shoot for — one which, when achieved, will leave us with a feeling of accomplishment, of having done the route in the right way? In other words, *what is the point of the game?* Every climb is different. A good standard which is always applicable and yet which also allows for the individuality of each route is our first ascent principle. It can guide us in questions of style as well as ethics. If we take for our general stylistic goal the way the first ascent was done, we have a ready-made, always available standard for a minimum style to shoot for. The acceptance of this principle has the advantage of obviating *general* style controversies. A further advantage is that the style of the first ascent is a reasonable goal, for those who come after have the psychological advantage of knowing the route will go, as well as a description of the route. If we regard the style in which a route was established, we pay respect to the men who did it, and show we are aware of their values and that we consider their climb a creation, not just another climb to be knocked off and checked in our guidebook.

Related Considerations

Use Nuts and Runners: A rockclimb is a fragile entity. Questions of style and ethics aside, the use of natural runners and artificial chockstones is desirable because they leave the rock intact. The damage pitons do is three-fold: they can make a route harder or easier thus changing its character, they create unsightly scars, and can dangerously loosen blocks and flakes. So even in cases where a first ascent involved pitons, we should minimize their use as they are destructive.

Litter: If you carry cans of food on climbs, smash the tins and take them to the top with you. Or better, use uncanned food such as salami, nuts, raisins, etc. Most organic matter can be readily disposed of, but orange rinds are best packed out as they are not eaten by animals and are slow to disintegrate.

Fixed Pitons: Popular climbing areas will often have some routes containing fixed pins. Usually these will be made of soft iron, except for the larger angles. These should be left in place.

photo by Liz Robbins

an apology

Writing this last chapter has been difficult and painful. It involves do's and don't's, obligations and responsibilities. Most climbers are individuals who love freedom — they climb because it makes them feel free. We may expect then, that having others suggest how they ought to climb will rub wrong. There used to be so few climbers that it didn't matter where one drove a piton, there wasn't a worry about demolishing the rock. Now things are different. There are so many of us, and there will be more. A simple equation exists between freedom and numbers: the more people, the less freedom. If we are to retain the beauties of the sport, the fine edge, the challenge, we must consider our style of climbing; and if we are not to mutilate and destroy the routes, we must eliminate the heavy-handed use of pitons and bolts.

APPENDIX
CLIMBING CLASSIFICATION SYSTEMS

To avoid getting in over our heads it is helpful to know the difficulty of routes, A climbing classification system is a shorthand method of describing this. Such systems provide divisions of difficulty and symbols for them, and place routes in the divisions most appropriate. These systems rate types of climbs and different aspects of the same climb. For example, in the National Climbing Classification System, one of the two principal American methods, routes are rated in three ways. One is the grade of the hardest free pitch, described with an "F" and numerals 1 to 10 for ascending degrees of difficulty. Another aspect rated in this system is the hardest aid pitch, by using an "A" and numerals 1 to 5. Finally, the "overall" or general difficulty or challenge of the route is graded with Roman numerals I to VI, with I being about a half-day affair and VI usually being a multi-day climb. Thus a climber of moderate ability might select a route graded NCCS III F6 A2, but he would avoid one rated III F9 A2. Or, if he were a good free climber, but had little experience in artificial, he might shun a II F7 A4 in favor of a II F9 A1. In this way, classification of routes helps us choose those consistent with our ability.

Nevertheless, although such systems are helpful in avoiding trouble, they require caution in use. First, there are different types of difficulty in free climbing. Rarely, for example, will an individual be as apt in slab climbing as in crack climbing. And ones ability will vary from day to day, according to mood and other variables. That one has, by virtue of a maximum effort on a good day, managed a difficult route, does not necessarily mean that all climbs of that grade are within ones grasp. In other words, take the classification of climbs with a certain amount of salt, and avoid a bad aftertaste.

Index